SEASONS SEASONS SEASONS SEASONS

SUMMER

Moira Butterfield

Illustrated by Helen James

FRANKLIN WATTS

LONDON • SYDNEY

☙ An Appleseed Editions book

First published in 2005 by Franklin Watts
96 Leonard Street, London EC2A 4XD

Franklin Watts Australia
Level 17/207 Kent Street, Sydney, NSW 2000

© 2005 Appleseed Editions

Designed and illustrated by Helen James
Edited by Mary-Jane Wilkins

ISBN 0 7496 6001 5

A CIP catalogue for this book is available from the British Library

Photographs by Corbis (Asian Art & Archaeology, Paul Barton, Ray Bird; Frank
Lane Picture Agency, E.O. Hoppé, Rob Howard, Martin Jones, Wolfgang Kaehler,
George D. Lepp, Chris Lisle, Robert Llewelyn, Buddy Mays, Ariel Skelley)

Printed and bound in Thailand

Contents

All about summer

Summer is a season, a time of year when the weather is warm. Most people love summer!

The sun gives us life. Without it there would be no animals or plants on our planet.

Our sizzling sun

We get warmth and light from the sun.
It is a huge fiery ball of burning gas.
Our Earth travels around the sun.
It takes one year to go all the
way around.

Earth words

The two halves of the world are called the northern and the southern hemispheres. While one has summer, the other has winter. The area around the middle of the world is called the equator.

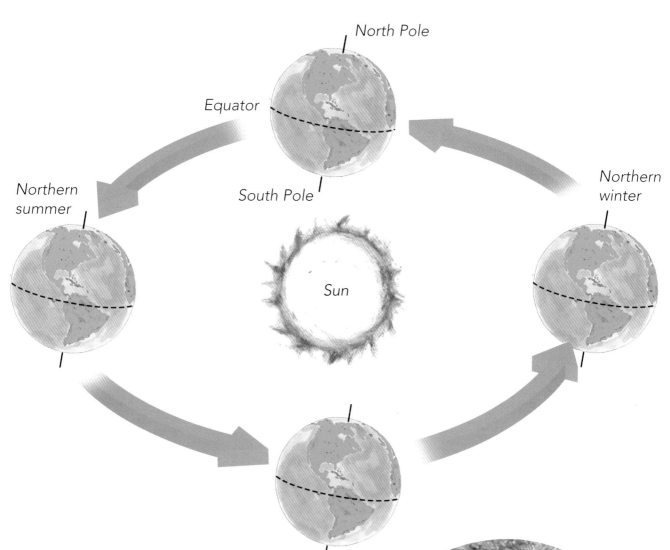

North Pole

Equator

South Pole

Northern
summer

Sun

Northern
winter

Summer or winter?

The Earth leans towards the sun as it
travels around it. The half nearest to the
sun has summer and the other half has
winter. So as the Earth gradually turns
around, the seasons change.

Poles stay cold

The far north and south of the Earth
are called the poles. They are never
near enough the sun to get really hot
in summer. They are always covered
in freezing ice.

5

My summer, your summer

Summer does not come at the same time for everyone. When it is summer for you, it is winter on the other side of the world.

Summer north and south

In the northern half of the Earth summer comes in June, July and August. In the southern half summer comes in December, January and February.

What about the middle?

In countries along the equator it is hot all year round. There is no winter or summer and places have wet and dry seasons instead.

Days and nights

As the Earth travels round the sun it spins in space like a top. It takes 24 hours to spin once. First one side faces the sun, then the other, giving us days and nights. In summer days are longer and nights shorter.

The hottest summer place in the northern hemisphere is the Sahara Desert in North Africa.

The equator has wet and dry seasons.

The hottest summer place in the southern hemisphere is Queensland, Australia.

Sun at bedtime

In the far north of the world, called the Arctic, the summer sun shines all day and all night. That is why it is called the land of the midnight sun.

Around the top of the world the Arctic sea freezes in winter and melts in summer. But the North Pole always stays frozen.

Summer snow

The far south of the world is called Antarctica. In summer the sun shines day and night, but never melts the snow. The sun's rays bounce off the snow and are so dazzling that anyone visiting has to wear sunglasses even though they are wrapped up warmly.

The summer sun shines at midnight near the North Pole.

Summer's coming

When summer comes the weather grows warmer and the days last longer. There is more time to play outside! Look out for these summer signs.

Who's buzzing?

Insects hatch in warm weather. You'll know summer is coming when you spot a butterfly or hear a buzzing bee. You might even get an itchy bite on your skin from a summer insect called a mosquito.

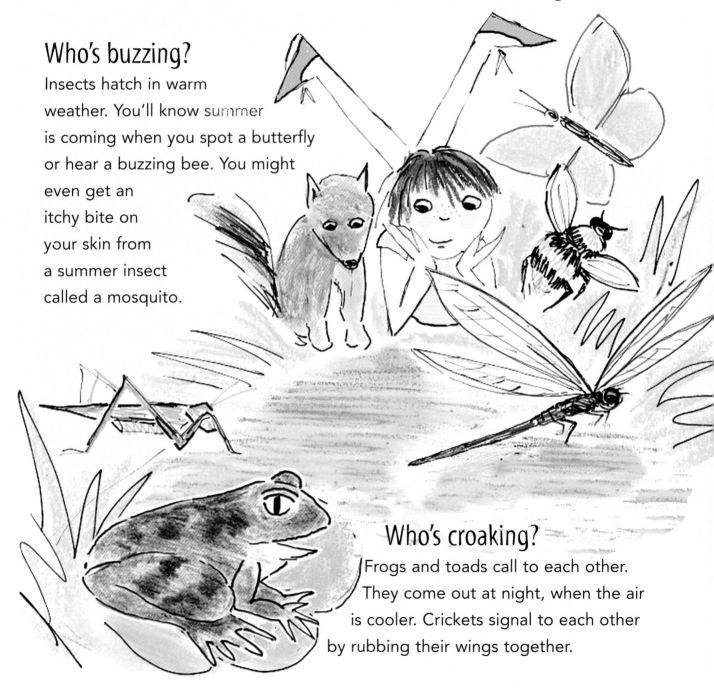

Who's croaking?

Frogs and toads call to each other. They come out at night, when the air is cooler. Crickets signal to each other by rubbing their wings together.

Can you feel summer?

You can feel summer coming because the temperature rises outside. We measure temperature with a thermometer that has coloured liquid inside it. The liquid squeezes up a thin tube as it gets warmer. Numbers along the tube measure how far up the liquid goes.

These numbers show the temperature, measured in degrees Celsius (°C) or degrees Fahrenheit (°F).

Can you see summer?

Sometimes you look into the distance and see that the air seems to be wobbling. This happens when the weather is hot and heat rises up from the ground.

Can you touch summer?

The summer sun heats up objects. Have you noticed how hot the seats in your car can be in summer? Touch them to feel some of the sun's power at your fingertips!

Summer and you

The temperature of the sun is hotter than the warmest oven or the fiercest fire. That's why you can feel its warmth even though it is 150 million kilometres away from you.

Water out, water in

Your skin has lots of tiny holes in it, called pores. When you get warm, water comes out of your body through your pores. The water evaporates, which means it disappears into the air. This helps to cool you down by taking some of your body heat away with it.

Slip on some shades

Strong summer sunlight can dazzle you so you need sunglasses to shield your eyes from the glare. Never look directly at the sun, even with sunglasses on. Its light is so strong it would damage your eyes forever.

In warm weather you need to drink lots of water to replace the water you lose through your pores.

Skin and sun

Skin has a substance called melanin inside it, to help protect it from burning by the sun. People with light skin have less melanin than people with dark skin so they burn more easily. Tanned skin makes extra melanin to try to protect itself from the strong summer sun.

The sun's rays can harm anyone's skin badly. In summer you should always wear sun lotion to protect you from burning, and a hat to shade your face and head.

Safe shade

The sun is hottest in the middle of the day, when it is high overhead. People in hot countries stay in the shade during the hottest hours. They know that the midday sun is dangerous because it is so strong.

Summer garden

In the summer garden the sun's heat helps plants to grow, flower and make fruit.

Leaves at work

A green leaf uses sunshine to help it make food.

1. First the leaf takes water from the ground and a gas called carbon dioxide from the air.

sunlight

2. The leaf uses sunlight and a green substance (called chlorophyll) to turn the water and the carbon dioxide into sugary food and a gas called oxygen.

oxygen

carbon dioxide

3. The leaf uses the food to grow bigger and sends the oxygen out into the air. The way a leaf makes food for itself is called photosynthesis.

roots take in water

Summer smells

Flowers smell sweet to attract insects. They have bright colours too. Some flowers even have lines and dots on them to guide insects to their store of nectar.

Flowers are for insects

In summer there are lots of insects around to feed on the nectar deep inside each flower.

When an insect climbs into a flower tiny pollen grains stick to its body. When it flies to another flower it carries the pollen with it.

A flower needs pollen from a similar flower to fertilize it. Then it goes on to grow fruit and seeds.

Following the sun

The petals of many flowers open in sunshine and close at night. Some flowers even move to face the sun wherever it is in the sky. That way they soak up as much sunshine as they can.

Sunflowers move around during the day to face the sun.

13

Summer farm

Farm crops and fruit grow and ripen in the sunshine.
A bowl of sweet summer fruit is delicious!

Crops for us

In summer you see fields of cereal plants growing tall in the sun. Wheat, oats and barley are all types of cereal. They are grown for their seeds, called grain. We use the grain to make food such as flour.

> Can you see the grains of this wheat? They are at the top.

See the summer harvest

In late summer crops are ready to harvest. You might see a big combine harvester cutting the cereal and separating the grains from the stalks. In some countries farmers cut their crops by hand, with a long knife called a scythe.

Yummy summer fruits

Once a flower has pollen from another flower, the summer sunshine helps it grow into a fruit. The fruit has seeds which might grow into a new plant.

Dried in sunshine

Some farmers grow crops that they dry in the sunshine to make food for us. Grapes are dried in the sun to make raisins. Tomatoes are dried in the sun to make them extra tasty.

Fruits to find

Fruits tempt animals to come and eat them. The animals carry away the fruit and help to spread the seeds to a new place. Soft fruit such as peaches, cherries, raspberries and strawberries are all ripe and juicy in summer.

The seed of a peach is inside the peach stone. It grows from a peach flower.

Summer animals

Summer is a busy time for animals.
There is a lot of food for them to gather.

Honey in the hive

Honey bees are busy in the summer. They live in groups, sometimes in man-made hives. The busiest bees are the worker bees. They make honey for baby bees (called larvae) to eat.

Every morning worker bees leave the hive to look for nectar. When they find some they take it to the hive, with some pollen. They carry pollen on their legs. The bees make nectar into honey and use pollen as food.

Sometimes you can see yellow pollen on the legs of worker bees.

16

Keeping cool

Humans are a kind of animal called a mammal. Mammals are animals with warm blood and the summer sunshine makes us even warmer. Some mammals, such as dogs, pant to cool down. The heat from their bodies comes out of their mouths. Some mammals, such as elephants, have very big ears. Lots of body heat comes out of them, like a radiator in a house.

Sun-bathing reptiles

Reptiles love the warm sun. They do not have warm blood as we mammals do. Instead they need sunshine to warm them from outside and give them energy to move around. In summer reptiles like to bask in the sunshine.

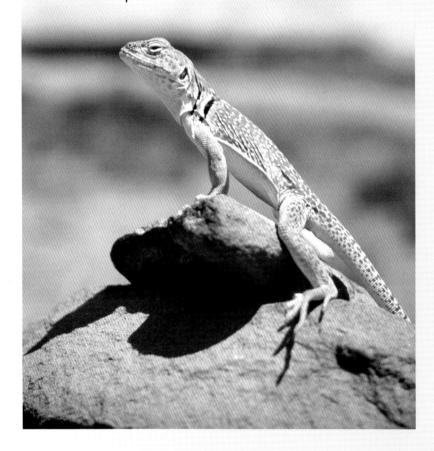

Lizards, snakes and crocodiles are all reptiles. They like to sunbathe.

Mammals like to stay in the shade when the sun is hot.

17

Hottest ever

The hottest summer places in the world are deserts.
They become baking hot during the daytime.

Nightlife

Desert animals usually hide in the shade during the day. They might shelter under rocks or burrow into sand. Most animals come out at night, when the temperature drops. Reptiles and insects are the most common animals in deserts.

Hottest in the world

One of the world's hottest summer desert places is Death Valley in California, USA.

Camel power

Camels are good at living in the desert, even in the blistering heat of summer. They can go without food and water for many days. Their feet are wide so they can walk along easily in soft sand.

When rain never comes

There is drought when no rain falls for a long time, if summer is longer and drier than normal. Water runs out and the ground dries up. Plants die and farmers lose their crops.

Drought can lead to famine. People and animals may starve when their food crops die.

A cloud of stinging sand

In sandy deserts the summer heat can whip up sand and dust into a sandstorm which blocks out the sun.

If you were caught in a sandstorm you would need to shelter, or the blowing sand would sting your skin and get into your eyes and mouth.

Summer stories

All over the world there are legends about the sun and summer. Here are some of them.

An Aborigine sun story

Good sky spirits make a fire in the sky every day. They collect firewood during the night and heap it up in the sky. Then they start the fire and the blaze lights up the Earth in the morning. By midday the fire is at its fiercest and hottest. Then it dies away until a few red embers are left glowing in the evening.

An Inuit sun story

The Inuit people of Greenland have a sun goddess called Malina. She quarrelled with her brother, the moon god Anningan, smeared dirt over his face and ran away across the sky. Her brother chases her, but never catches her. That is why the sun, then the moon appear above us.

A Chinese sun story

In Chinese legend light and dark are always fighting. Sometimes dark gets the upper hand. Then the Earth has longer nights. In summer light is winning the fight, and that's why the days are longer.

A Japanese sun legend

Amaterasu is a Japanese sun goddess. She argued so badly with her brother that she hid in a cave and the Earth was plunged into darkness. Then the other gods thought of a way to persuade her to come out. They held a party outside the entrance, and placed a big mirror on a tree nearby. Hearing the party, Amaterasu peeped out and was so fascinated to see herself in the mirror she came outside again, filling the world with light.

21

Summer parties

People celebrate summer with special parties. Here are some of them.

Solstice parties

In northern lands 21 June is the longest day of the year. It is called the summer solstice. In Finland there are 23 hours of daylight and everyone joins in a bonfire party called Johannus. They decorate their homes with flowers and birch branches.

In southern lands 21 December is the summer solstice, the longest day. It's a good time to hold parties and barbecues.

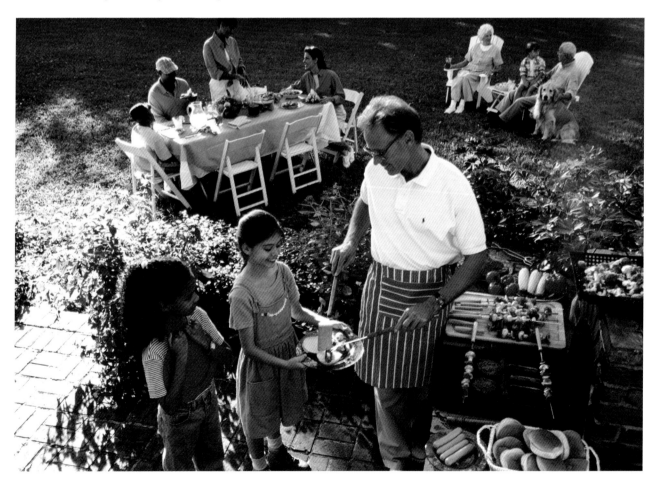

Sun festival

In Peru 24 June marks Inti Raymi, the ancient Inca festival of the sun. It is still celebrated in the city of Cuzco, where the sun god is honoured with music and dancing at the ancient sun temple.

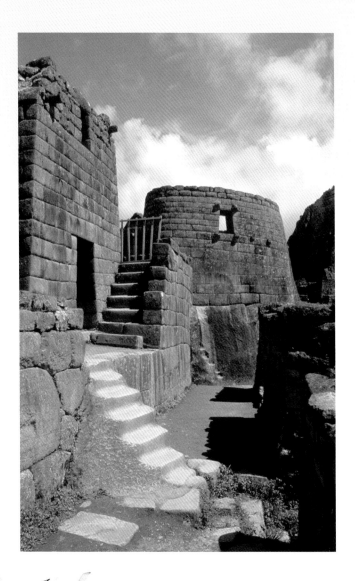

Thanks for food

In Accra, a town in Ghana, Africa, the people of the Ga tribe celebrate their August harvest with the Homowo festival. Homowo means making fun of hunger. It's a big party, with dancing and drumming to thank the gods for the crops.

Summer dance

Traditionally native North American tribes celebrate the summer corn harvest with a Green Corn Festival, to thank the creator of the world for providing food. Sometimes they do a green corn celebration dance.

23

Paint the summer

Here are some ideas for making summery pictures.

Make your picture hot

Use warm colours to paint a summer picture. Try shades of yellow, red and orange. They are the colour of the sun and fire.

Put blue and yellow together to make a picture that looks full of sunlight.

Bright yellow next to bright blue in a picture makes the light look bright, just like in summer.

Summer shadows

When the sun shines brightly on things they throw a shadow, so put some shadows in your summer pictures. Here are some rules to follow.

Sun lights up one side of an object but not the other. You can show this by adding some darker colour.

Think about where the sunlight is coming from in your picture. A shadow falls on the ground away from the sun.

24

Paint a summer sunset

A good way to paint a warm glowing sunset is to use wet paper, so the colours run together. You need thick white paper, masking tape, a pot of water, some poster paints and brushes.

1. Tape the paper down flat on a table or board. Then paint all over it with clean water.

2. Paint watery yellow over the paper. Then paint watery red streaks across the yellow. The paints will run together.

3. Put a line of darker watery blue along the top, then leave your picture to dry.

4. Paint in the sun, and add some ground at the bottom of your picture.

Another way to make a glowing sunset picture is to glue torn strips of yellow, orange and red tissue paper across a page so they overlap each other.

25

Make a piece of summer

Make your own hat to keep off the sun
or a pretty seed necklace.

Chinese summer hat

In China some farmers wear cone-shaped hats to work in the fields.
To make one you need a big piece of stiff paper or thin card that
measures about 50 cm square, a ruler, a pencil, scissors and sticky tape.

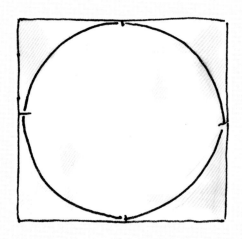

*It doesn't matter
if the circle isn't
exactly right. You
can trim it later.*

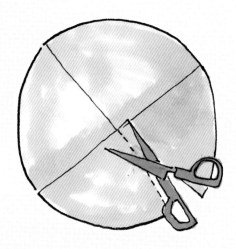

1. Draw a circle 50 cm wide by marking
the middle point of each side, then
joining the marks with curved lines.

2. Fold the circle in half, then in half
again. Unfold it and cut along one
of the folds to the middle.

3. Overlap the cut edges to make
a shallow cone-shape. Tape them
underneath and then check the
cone fits your head.

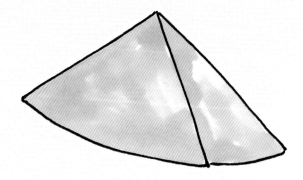

4. Decorate your hat with tissue, crepe paper, string or paint. Tape on two ribbons to tie under your chin.

Fruit seed jewellery

You can make necklaces or bracelets from melon seeds. You need a tray, a thick needle, some thread and an adult to help.

1. Scoop out the melon seeds and wash them. Put them on a tray and dry them in a warm cupboard or out in the sun.

2. Thread the needle and knot the end of the thread. Pierce each melon seed and pull the thread through it.

3. When you have finished knot the ends of the thread tightly together.

Be a summer scientist

These summer experiments will help you discover the mystery of shadows and how much plants need sunlight.

Solve the shadow mystery

Do shadows change or stay the same? Make a cardboard shadow man to find the answer. You will need some card, coloured pencils, a sheet of white paper, some sticky tape and a compass, as well as a sunny day.

1. Draw and cut out a man shape from card. Leave extra card along the bottom to fold back so he stands up. Tape him on to white paper.

2. Early on a sunny morning, take the shadow man outside and put him down facing south. Draw round his shadow, and write down the time.

3. Take the man outside again later and draw round his shadow in a different colour. Write down the time. Do this a third time later.

4. Look at the three lines you have drawn. You will see that the shadow changes its position and its length during the day. Which is the shortest shadow?

28

Do plants need sunlight?

Find out whether plants need sunlight with two old dry potatoes that are just beginning to sprout.

1. Put one potato in a dark cupboard, and the other potato on a sunny windowsill.

2. After a few days look to see what is happening. Which has healthy green shoots and which has weak pale shoots?

The difference between the two potatoes is sunlight. It has helped the one on the windowsill grow healthy shoots.

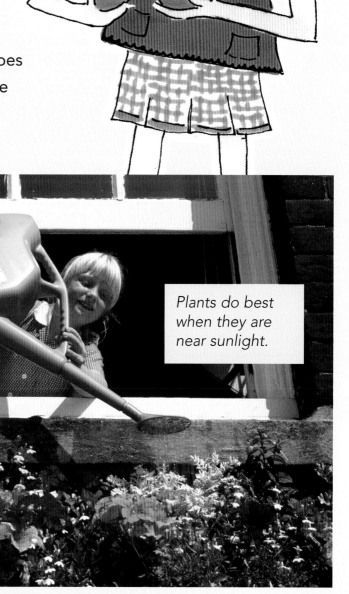

Plants do best when they are near sunlight.

Words to remember

crops Plants that farmers grow and harvest.

desert A place that is very dry. In summer deserts can be baking hot.

drought A water shortage that happens if there is no rain for a long time.

equator The imaginary line around the middle of the Earth.

evaporation Water disappearing into the air. Hot sun makes water evaporate.

hemispheres The northern and southern halves of the world.

land of the midnight sun The far north of the world, where the sun shines day and night during summer.

melanin A substance in your skin that helps to protect you from damaging sunrays.

nectar The sweet liquid inside a flower. Bees make honey from nectar.

photosynthesis Something that happens when a green leaf collects water and a gas called carbon dioxide, then makes them into plant food and oxygen. To do this the leaf needs sunlight and a green substance called chlorophyll.

pollen Tiny grains inside a flower. A flower needs pollen grains from another similar flower before it can grow fruit and seeds.

season A time of year that has a particular kind of weather and temperature.

summer solstice The longest day of the year. In the north it is 21 June. In the south it is 21 December.

temperature How hot or cold something is.

thermometer A tube with liquid inside which measures temperature.

Index